Yelenica,

Thank you
so much!

"JORDAN CHANEY'S TEACHING IS INSIGHTFUL, practical, and accessible—and like any good teacher, he's interested in helping both the artist and the person. 'Perform your Spoken Word poem for a live audience!' is the last task in Art of the Spoken Word, and that endnote underscores an important lesson—among many—of this book: Connect with others! Don't be afraid. Put yourself out there! Chaney knows poetry—lives poetry—and his enthusiasm is contagious in these pages."

Tod Marshall, Washington State Poet Laureate

ART OF THE SPOKEN WORD

For more information or to book Jordan Chaney to facilitate
a workshop with your students or youth group contact him at
jordanchaneypoet@gmail.com.

TABLE OF CONTENTS

Section 1. Communication

The goal of communication

Section 2. Creativity

The power of creativity

Section 3. Confidence

What is confidence?

A short story...

In the winter of 2004 I entered a few poems that I had written into a poetry contest in Seattle, WA. But it wasn't just any poetry contest — it was a slam. Slam is performance art. It's live theater mixed with language arts, mixed with public speaking, mixed with fire, courage, truth, joy, and pain. Slam is raw, it's honest, and it's a beautiful and wild art form that has created an entirely new way for poets to get their message across! It's not what you expect, but it's everything you want it to be!

The Washington Poets Association and Bart Baxter, an MTV award-winning slam Poet, chose me as one of the finalist for their slam. It was an honor, but I was terrified! I had never performed my real poetry in front of real people before and on top of that, this was a competition — judges holding big white scorecards, critiquing every word and gesture. It was undoubtedly one of the scariest, most rewarding, and life-changing experiences of my life.

That was 11 years ago, and since then I have spoken and performed for well over 250,000 people across the United States and even in Athens, Greece. I was chosen to attend a writer's workshop in Big Sur, California with The Sun Magazine where I learned from some of the greatest writers in the world! I've written two poetry collections and today I help others overcome their fears of public speaking and create poetic works of art that inspire, challenge and even rescue. A majority of the lessons and experiences that I've learned as a poet are compiled in this workbook, Art of the Spoken Word.

Poetry is a superpower. It saved my life. I have seen it save many lives in various ways. The ability to creatively communicate one's innermost thoughts and feelings, demons and angels, is a brave journey of self-discovery. And whether we choose to take on that task with poetry or some other medium, we all, at some point, must do just that — conquer ourselves to create ourselves...

A note on knowledge

The Great Ancient Pyramids of Egypt were built over 7000 years ago with such advanced knowledge and skill that they are still standing to this day.

The attainment of Knowledge is similar to building a Pyramid.

If you start with a solid base and set each mud-brick firmly so that you can build upon it, eventually you will have attained a structure that even time itself may not be able to conquer.

Knowledge truly is power.
Creative communication is a superpower.

The following lessons are laid out brick by brick so that you are able to attain a firm grasp on the Art of the Spoken Word.

The final stone set, the capstone, will be the moment when you can confidently perform an original Spoken Word Poem in front of a
Live Audience.

And may the elements tremble in your presence...

Jordan

INTRODUCE YOURSELF.

Write a 100-word biography about where you're from,
where you're at and where you're going in life…

_____
_____
_____
_____
_____
_____
_____
_____
_____
_____
_____
_____
_____
_____
_____
_____
_____
_____
_____
_____
_____
_____
_____

The end.

1

COMMUNICATION

THE GOAL OF COMMUNICATION

The goal of communication is to transfer a message, an idea, a thought, an emotion, or all four of those, to another person or group of people.

We use words to transfer messages, ideas, thoughts, and emotions.

So, what are words?

Words are pictures.

They are a verbal or written representation of the physical world.

Think about it!

Every word that you know or understand creates a picture in your mind. If you hear or read the word moon, a picture of a moon will appear in your mind. Therefore all words, in some way, shape, or form are pictures.

Spoken words are verbal pictures.
Written words are symbolic pictures.

In order to successfully communicate with someone it is mandatory that both people know or understand the word or words being used to communicate. If both people don't know the word or words then communication doesn't actually take place.

When we don't understand someone it is because we are not familiar with the words they are using. In other words, we don't see the pictures they are trying to transfer into our mind. To get better at this, use a dictionary and define any words in this book that are new to you.

WORDS ARE PICTURES

KNOWLEDGE CHECK!

1. What is the goal of communication?

2. Why do we use words?

3. What are words?

*The following exercises will help you understand this concept better

LESSON 1

4 Minutes to Telepathy & The Lego Exercise

In this lesson, you will learn the importance of silent eye contact, how to overcome communication anxiety, how basic small talk gets us by, and what it means to communicate your words (pictures) with clarity and intention.

4 MINUTES TO TELEPATHY

THE PURPOSE:

To examine and demonstrate four different aspects of communication through four 1-minute exercises, including but not limited to eye contact, overcoming the fear of public speaking, social anxiety, and practicing "telepathy" to communicate with intention.

THE IDEA:

This activity involves two people sitting across from each other and completing the timed exercises to the best of their verbal and non-verbal communication abilities. The goal is to improve our ability to communicate our thoughts, ideas, and emotions with clarity and intention.

YOU WILL NEED:

2 people, 2 chairs, a table, and a timer. Throughout the following exercises both participants will sit facing each other 8 inches apart.

INSTRUCTIONS:

Level 1. Silent eye contact –keep silent eye contact with your partner for 60 seconds.

Level 2. Gibberish –speak in a made up language or gibberish with your partner for 60 seconds.

Level 3. Small talk –have a conversation about anything you choose with your partner for 60 seconds.

Level 4. Telepathy –practice telepathy with partner for 60 seconds. (find directions on next page)

TELEPATHY DIRECTIONS

1. While sitting across from your partner decide who will go first, Person A or Person B. Establish the sender and the receiver.

2. Person A informs Person B that he/she is thinking of a number between 1 and 10.

3. Person A visualizes this number; he/she actually sees it in the form of a mental image picture in their mind either written on a piece of paper, or spelled out in the air in front of them, or even as a picture text message.

4. Once Person A has mentally seen and visualized their number, he/she imagines the number floating from their forehead and into Person B's forehead.

5. After completing this visualization process Person A says "Sent" to Person B, informing them that they have telepathically transmitted the chosen number.

6. Person B then goes with their gut — their first impression of what they believe the number is — and informs Person A instantly. (remember, this is not guesswork, go with your gut!)

7. Person A and Person B go back and forth for 60 seconds alternating as sender and receiver.

"The single biggest problem in communication is the illusion that it has taken place."

- George Bernard Shaw

In this next exercise you will discover just how much you **DO NOT** actually say when you communicate and the kinds of problems that can cause!

LEGO EXERCISE

The Purpose:

To enhance the ability of transferring pictures from our mind into another person's mind. In other words, we are enhancing our ability to communicate clearly.

The Idea:

The builder and instructor have 10 minutes to put the Legos together with as much accuracy as possible. The builder is not allowed to see the instructions and the instructor is not allowed to see the Legos.

You will need:

Legos, Lego instructions, a timer, 2 chairs, and a table

Instructions:

Step 1. Person A and Person B decide who will be the builder and who will be the instructor.

Step 2. Now, the builder and instructor sit back to back in chairs. The builder will use the table to build the Legos.

Step 3. The instructor holds on to the instructions. The builder holds on to the Legos.

Step 4. Set the timer for 10 minutes. And GO!

Breaking down each round of 4 Minutes to Telepathy and The Lego Exercise

Silent Eye Contact

Maintaining silence with another person allows you to be receptive to whatever the other person is trying to communicate to you. Maintaining eye contact is a sign of confidence and respect when someone is speaking to you and when you are speaking to an audience.

Gibberish

The purpose of the gibberish round is to help a person overcome the fear of sounding foolish or making mistakes while they speak or perform in front of an audience. We instinctively know that speaking aloud reveals all kinds of things about ourselves that others wouldn't otherwise know had we not opened our mouths. Overcoming the fear of making speech mistakes will help us speak freely.

Small Talk

Engaging in basic conversations is a simple social skill that we may not realize is a difficult task for some. It can stem from lack of confidence or low self-esteem. It can also come from fear of sounding foolish or fear of rejection. Engaging in small talk with an audience will put both you and them at ease and allow you to deliver without anxiety.

Telepathy

The telepathy round is not necessarily meant to grant a person superhuman powers, but wouldn't that be nice?! The telepathy round is meant to help a person communicate with clarity and intention and to bring all of the previous rounds into play. Sending and receiving communication takes confidence, eye contact, and intention.

The Lego Exercise

The Lego Exercise is almost a reversal of all the other exercises. Here we attempt to master transferring words (pictures) without eye contact, and with a timer set to create pressure and anxiety! This puts pressure on the 2 people to apply speaking with clarity and intention and shows how communication takes teamwork!

4 Minutes to Telepathy & Lego Exercise

1. Why is Silent Eye Contact important when communicating with others?

_____

_____

_____

2. What is the purpose of the Gibberish round?

_____

_____

_____

3. How can Small Talk help a speaker or performer?

_____

_____

_____

4. What does the Telepathy round help a person do?

_____

_____

_____

5. What does The Lego Exercise attempt to master?

_____

_____

_____

_____

LESSON 2

Unification, Message, and Metaphor
Bad Poetry vs. Good Poetry

In this lesson, you will learn about the 3 elements that make a poem good and why people consider certain poetry to be bad.

UNIFICATION, MESSAGE, AND METAPHOR

1. <u>Unification:</u> Make connections; tie it all together!

Unification is the process of being united or made into a whole.

Example: 4 tires, an engine, a windshield are all <u>parts</u> that when 'unified' make up a <u>whole</u> car.

There are obviously more parts to a car, but the point is this: when you are writing and want to get a point across it helps to write so that all of the parts of your body of writing support the whole or the central idea. That is good communication or quality writing.

2. <u>Message:</u> What are you trying to say?

This is a significant point you're trying to make or the central theme of your writing. It could be political, social, moral, or even spiritual.

Example: It could be something as simple as "I love pancakes" to something as complex as "Systemic oppression is the fundamental reason for a majority of society's racial and economic disparities."

3. <u>Metaphor:</u> Say it in a different way...

Metaphor is figure of speech, image, analogy, comparison, symbol, and/or personification.

"Metaphor is the lifeblood of all art." –Twyla Tharp, Choreographer

Example: I cried as much as I possibly could that day in fact I became the ocean I sobbed seahorses and starfish I wailed with the whales I wept so much I made Poseidon blush my chest opened like the ocean and the whirlpools swallowed all of my secret slave ships up and it freed me!

*None of the above is literally true. However, all of the above is 100% true, metaphorically. A metaphor is basically taking 1 thing/ idea and saying it in a different way or many different ways to get an idea across creatively.

Good poetry will CONNECT all three of these.

CONNECTION VS. NON-SEQUITUR

Whether you're writing poems, raps or speeches, if you want to be effective and connect with your audience then it's imperative that you make your artwork connect in some way.

Lets take a look at the definitions of connection and non-sequitur in action below...

Connection – a relationship in which a person, thing, or
idea is linked or associated with something else
(when two or more things are similar)

Non-sequitur – a conclusion or statement that doesn't logically
follow from the previous argument or statement
(something random that doesn't fit)

Which word below doesn't belong?

watermelon apple banana pear shoe

If you answered shoe you are correct.
Shoe is the obvious word that does not fit.
The other words are all fruits and are edible.
A shoe is something you wear on your foot.

Ok lets take it up a notch!

Which word below doesn't belong?

watermelon apple banana monkey skyscraper ocean

If you answered ocean you are correct.
Watermelon, apple, and banana are fruits.
Banana, monkey, and skyscraper connect as follows:
Bananas are eaten by monkeys, monkeys are like
gorillas in a way, king kong is a gorilla that climbed a skyscraper.
Ocean has no obvious connection in the group of words

Make the following random words connect in a short poem.
Include a message of some kind!

cloud · wristwatch · pearls · blue · truth · construct · bus · choice

_____
_____
_____
_____
_____
_____
_____
_____
_____
_____
_____
_____
_____
_____
_____
_____
_____
_____
_____
_____
_____
_____
_____
_____
_____

Once you have finished, share your poem with your partner
or group and quiz them to see if they can spot connections,
(non-sequitur, if any) and the message!

BAD POETRY vs. GOOD POETRY

I'll say it here just so it's been said: poetry, whether it's considered bad or good, is all in the eye or ear of the beholder. There really is no such thing as bad or good poetry as long as it has an admirer, but for the sake of this lesson we are going to say that bad poetry is poetry that doesn't reach the goal of communication which is **to transfer a message, an idea, a thought, an emotion, or all four of these, to another person or group of people.** Good poetry will communicate some or all of these.

Below are a few exercises that will help you grasp this concept better.

Your goal will be to determine if the poem communicates.

Exercise: Bad Poetry

A bad poem will make no clear sense and have no clear message. The words will NOT unify or connect and the poem will NOT convey any real understandable meaning. This is what we will call bad poetry.

This first poem "The oh yeah" is made up of the following random words:

honey green blue teal love diamond meadow
bright green Norway white as cake brown

The oh yeah

The honey began to drizzle
all the way up into a meadow
white as cake and brown as love.
There was a diamond,
not very bright but it was
teal as green little skittles.
Oh yeah and Norway.

Answer the following questions about the poem "The oh yeah".

1. What words unified or connected?

_____

_____

2. What is the message in this poem?

_____

_____

3. What ideas, thoughts, or emotions did you gather from the poem?

_____

_____

4. Were there any metaphors used? If so, what were they?

_____

_____

_____

Now if you have studied the lessons correctly so far answering the above questions should have been fairly easy. The poem "The oh yeah" made no sense and had no clear message and that was the point of the exercise! The only thing that connected was the title and the words "oh yeah" in the last sentence. This illustrates what "bad poetry" or no communication looks like.

Exercise

Using the same random words: (honey green blue teal love diamond meadow bright green Norway white as cake brown)

Write bad poetry.

_____

_____

_____

_____

_____

_____

_____

Exercise: Good Poetry

A good poem should **transfer a message, an idea, a thought, an emotion, or all four of these, to another person or group of people.** But, keep in mind, even if a poem does do all of these things it doesn't necessarily mean it's going to be liked by everyone, that is a matter of taste and it's a whole other subject. But for the sake of argument we will say that good poetry communicates these things in some way.

This second poem "Paradise" was also made from random words. Study the random words; find them along with other connecting words in the poem.

sky happy awesome zebra love crunchy
red yellow enthusiasm rainbow meadow pretty

Paradise

Above a pretty meadow all the colors of the rainbow could be seen in the awesome sky. Red, yellow, you name it! The entire seen was alive with enthusiasm; every animal in the jungle ran wild, cheetahs zipped through the crunchy brush, monkeys swooshed and swung from the trees like trapeze artist, zebra's galloped over guppies guzzling gallons of rain drops that gathered in elephant foot prints left behind. The parrots and parakeets flew freely over the greenery, diving in and out of the clouds, completely in love with paradise.

What is the message in "Paradise"?

_____

_____

What words unified or connected in the poem? (list all that you find)

_____

_____

_____

_____

_____

_____

_____

_____

Exercise: message, metaphor and connections

Read the poem "Pond", and then circle all the words or ideas in the poem that you think connect with the title of the poem.

Pond

in a windswept desert

where all life appears to
have perished and all is

      barren
bleak
           and
treeless

where lush thick plants have
drawn their last sips from the soil
then shriveled back into the sand
the way dung beetles burrow

somehow

there you are

overflowing

bulging at the banks

        with

           life

What do you think the message and the metaphor are?

_____
_____
_____
_____

Exercise: find the message and metaphor

What is the message and what is the metaphor in the following poem?

_____

_____

_____

_____

TIME MACHINE

Cause I can see it now…
Way out in the far reaches of my finite life;
sixty or so years from today.
Where the baby I once was has come
to know its own wrinkles once again.
When cars hover and everything is all
shiny, white and smooth.
When what hair I would have
is as silver as space suits.
When my joints ache and my bones squeak.
I'm gonna have an ugly green sweater with holes in it,
it's gonna be my favorite one too,
the one that I wear on lazy Sunday afternoons,
catching siestas in a rocking chair on
a large porch somewhere out there
cozily being lulled
to sleep by my own
last breaths…

That day will come.

So today I pretend.
I act as if I was given
a second chance to live.
That I traveled back from
that moment, to right here
and now, to do it all
over again.

Unification, Message, And Metaphor | Bad Poetry vs. Good Poetry

1. What is unification?

_____

_____

2. What is a metaphor?

_____

_____

_____

3. In this lesson, what is considered bad poetry?

_____

_____

_____

4. In this lesson, what is considered good poetry?

_____

_____

_____

5. Is there really such a thing as bad poetry?

_____

_____

6. What does non-sequitur mean?

_____

_____

_____

LESSON 3

Haiku & The 3 C's:
Playing with the sound of your voice

In this lesson, you will learn how to write haiku and
to give your spoken words life by using "The 3 C's"!

HAIKU

Haiku is not a rhyme, but it can rhyme.

Haiku is a Japanese poem of seventeen syllables, in three lines of five, seven, and five, traditionally evoking images of the natural world.

(example below)

Scar Haiku

two guys versus one
they split my nose wide open
still, I stood my ground

Write a haiku.

The 3 C's
Caesura, Cadence, and Crescendo

Definitions of The 3 C's

Caesura -a poetic pause
Cadence -rhythm
Crescendo -a progressive increase in force or intensity

Verbal exercise: Apply The 3 C's to numbers

Line 1

Deliver in plain rhythm and place a **caesura** between each number

1(pause)2(pause)3(pause)4(pause)5(pause)

Line 2

Deliver in a whisper with an equal **cadence** between each number

1—2—3—4—5—7

Line 3

Deliver with **crescendo** followed by caesura

1 2 3 4 5(pause) 7

"The music is not in notes, but the silence in between." -Mozart

Verbal exercise: Apply The 3 C's to your haiku

Instructions:
Rewrite each line of your haiku in the spaces below, 1 line in each section. Then read each line aloud while implementing "The C" that applies.

Line 1

Deliver in a plain rhythm and place a **caesura** between each word

_____

Line 2

Deliver in a whisper with an equal **cadence** between each word

_____

Line 3

Deliver with **crescendo** followed by caesura

_____

When someone speaks in a monotonous tone
(a boring, non rhythmic tone) they will lose their listener.

Caesura, cadence, and crescendo are sonic paintbrushes,
meaning they give verbal communication color, texture, and life.

Apply them and you will captivate an audience. Fail to
use them and you will perform to a tsunami of yawns.

Playing with the sound of your voice...

       Below are 10 different ways to recite your haiku. The purpose of this exercise is to play with sound and to see what kind of impact each method can have on the spoken word. The idea here is to inject emotion or animation into your words. You wouldn't necessarily use these suggestions below in a live reading, though you could if the poem called for it. Put a check mark next to each one after you complete it!

o   Read your poem in a very boring, dry, and monotonous tone

o   Read your poem as if you were growing very angry

o   Rock a baby to sleep with your poem

o   Read your poem in super slow motion

o   Read your poem as fast as you can

o   Shout your poem from the mountaintops

o   Whisper your poem as if it were a secret

o   Read your poem as if it were your last words

o   Read your poem as if it were the saddest news you've ever read

o   Read the poem as if you just won the lottery

Haiku & The 3 C's

1. What is a haiku?

_____

_____

_____

2. In your own words, describe caesura:

_____

_____

_____

3. In your own words, describe cadence:

_____

_____

_____

4. In your own words, describe crescendo:

_____

_____

_____

5. What happens when someone speaks in a monotonous tone?

_____

_____

_____

LESSON 4

Rhyming 101: Couplets, Sonnets, and Raps

In this lesson, you will learn the basics of rhyme and discover those basic elements in everything from writing couplets and sonnets to writing raps!

RHYMING 101

Rhymes

Rhymes are words that have a matching or similar sound to them. Rhymes come especially handy when we're writing poetry or rap. If you would like **ample examples** or all kinds of **samples** then read this whole chapter cause there is more than a **handful**.

Above there are 4 words in bold. Ample, examples, samples, and handful.

Ample, examples and samples all rhyme with one another as end rhymes; the very last syllable of the word is "ample".

The last word "handful" rhymes in a different way. This is called assonance.

Assonance is the repetition of vowel sounds without the repetition of consonant sounds.

ample examples samples handful

The underlined parts of the words above match or rhyme because of vowels; that is what we consider assonance.

Consonants are the basic speech sounds, a letter or few letters connected to a vowel.

ample example samples handful

The underlined parts of the words above are the consonants. They are the beginning part of a word and in basic rhyme should not match the beginning part of word that you want to rhyme with it. For instance the word cat does not rhyme with the word cat, because cat and cat are the same word. In order for words to rhyme there has to be a changing up of consonants.

Rhyming Exercise

Rhyme using assonance – vowel sounds

Example: Here is a list of words that rhyme with the word *Monster*

roster, conquer, imposter, foster, lobster, mobster, stopper, mocker, locker...

I could go on. I could start using 2 words that are 1 syllable each that will rhyme with *Monster*. With enough practice, anything is possible with rhyming!

Using assonance, rhyme as many words as you can with the word *Party*.

_____

_____

_____

_____

_____

_____

_____

_____

_____

_____

_____

_____

_____

_____

Rhyming 101 Review

1. What is a rhyme?

_____

_____

_____

2. List 4 words that rhyme with the word bubble:

_____

_____

3. What is assonance?

_____

_____

_____

4. Using assonance, rhyme 4 words with the word mouth:

_____

_____

5. Why doesn't the word cat rhyme with the word cat?

_____

_____

_____

_____

In the next few pages, we will take a look at a few different classical and urban forms of rhyme and try it ourselves.

COUPLETS

Couplets are rhymes.

A couplet is 2 lines of rhyme; each line is the same measurement/meter.

Below are a few examples.

Most people do not know the sort of true story
of how Dr. Seuss rose to fortune, fame and glory.

This is the tall tale of an M.C. not afraid to try
and 2 of his homeboys that always stuck by.

Write a couplet.

_____

_____

_____

_____

_____

_____

_____

SONNETS

Sonnets are rhymes.

A sonnet is a 14-line poem that has 10 syllables per line and is written in 4 sections, also known as a quatrain. The first 3 quatrains consist of 4 lines each and have an alternating rhyme pattern and the last 2 lines rhyme with one another.

Here is an example of the rhyme patterns of a sonnet:

ABAB / CDCD / EFEF / GG

The following sentence is a line from one of the most famous sonnets in the world written by William Shakespeare (Sonnet 16). Underneath this line there are numbers demonstrating the syllable count per word. Note that the entire line equals 10 syllables.

Shall I compare thee to a summer's day
  1   1   2   1 1   2   1 = 10 syllables

The first quatrain is 4 alternating rhyming lines ABAB that establish the subject of the sonnet.

The second quatrain is 4 alternating rhyming lines CDCD that expand on the message of the sonnet.

The third quatrain is 4 alternating rhyming lines EFEF that complete the main message of the sonnet.

The fourth quatrain is 2 lines that rhyme with one another GG and conclude the sonnet.

Below are 2 examples to help you get a better idea of this style of poem.

Example 1

Chosen

1. You're a water-walker that parts the seas
2. with a thousand watt halo glowing crown
3. Golden lotus flowers around your feet
4. I prostrate self at your shrine, head on ground

5. Robed in loin cloth, on knees, ribs bear, exposed
6. fasting, craving, waiting, longing for love
7. Built a bon fire from god's verse and prose
8. tying my prayers to birds sailing above

9. For love I'd give my soul as offering
10. I would push the worlds back to Pangea
11. Cause love is glue for broken pottery
12. you're the perfect mix goddess and diva

13. I'm holy, awakened, I am the one
14. cause when in love you are enlightened, sun

Example 2

Mix Tape Sonnet

1. Shall I compare thee to a fresh mix tape?
2. You are way live'r, and lovelier too.
3. Your records spin softly –the needle meets fate,
4. Music fills a room with love and perfume.

5. For all the words I'd lost; escaped my tongue,
6. For all the notes I could not hit myself,
7. Your reflection in a playlist unsung,
8. And so I string them up like pearls to help.

9. Miles Davis and John Coltrane to start,
10. Some Lauryn Hill to bring back the 90's.
11. It's instrumental to expand one's heart;
12. A bouquet of dope songs to remind thee –

13. As long as the gods rule and their art reigns,
14. Men will always have the right words to say.

Write a sonnet.

RAP

Rap is rhyme.

Rap or Hip-hop "is an artistic and socio-political movement/culture that sprang from the disparate ghettos of New York in the early 70's coming off the heels of the Civil Rights Movement and approaching the end of the Vietnam war..."

–Q-Tip from Tribe Called Quest

Rap has become one of the most popular musical genres in the world. A rap can be as long or as short as the artist wants it to be. The rhyme scheme of a rap has almost no rules other than the rules of communication discussed earlier in this workbook.

In a typical rap song one line of rap is called a "bar" and the rhythm of that line will match with the beat cycle that the rap is written for. Usually one verse of rap is 16 bars or lines, and is not limited to any one rhyme scheme.

Example: a rap that mixes end rhyme and assonance

Love her rap

1. hard to believe that I'm fallin' for her so quickly
2. lost in her presence what a blessing after only a week
3. learning a lesson about love and life and how to be
4. accepting of the gifts that life keeps on giving to me
5. I'm hearing its message loud and clear so its hard to speak
6. her whole essence is holy I'm blind trying to see
7. where this could go ya never know when love is trying to free
8. you from where ever you've been and where its tryin' to lead you
9. been down some really dark paths and I couldn't see
10. the good or bad in any girl that would be right for me
11. she said he was just a friend I tried to believe it
12. he said she was lying and now im caught in between
13. that ol he say she say, the lies and deceit
14. I delete that replay no more past on repeat
15. You can keep all of your secrets and your dirty schemes
16. Its reality I may have found the girl of my dreams

Write a rap.

Poetry & Rap

1. What is a couplet?

_____

_____

_____

2. How many syllables are in each line of a sonnet?

_____

_____

3. How many lines of poetry are there in a sonnet?

_____

_____

4. How many bars equal 1 line of rap?

_____

_____

5. How many lines does a typical rap verse consist of?

_____

_____

REAL WORLD CHALLENGE!

Knowledge and Application make up 360° of education. In this challenge, apply what you have learned from this section.

1. Memorize the haiku that you wrote from this section.

2. Call a friend or family member and read it to them.

3. Read your poem to someone while making eye contact.

SECTiON 1 WRAP UP...

Now that we've learned a few basics in communication, poetry, and rhyme, lets move on to the next section and explore how creativity can move entire worlds.

2

CREATIVITY

THE POWER OF CREATIVITY

Creativity is the masterful wielding of the imagination onto the physical world.

I don't have any links or articles that can back up what I'm about to say but I'll say it boldly: ART SAVES LIVES. Art cures drug addictions, makes better mothers and fathers, it lifts communities up, keeps youths out of prison, helps youngsters graduate from high school, and sends poor kids to college. Art yanks the collar of the potential suicide jumper, and pulls him or her off the ledge. I am speaking not only from experience, but also from the experience of brave individuals that have shared their inspiring stories with me. Their stories serve as a testament to the power of art and creativity.

I am a poet. I use my craft in as many ways as I possibly can. Aside from this book, I perform poetry, teach others how to write it, I mentor youth, and I deliver motivational presentations. I have even traveled the United States and the world practicing what I love. On a regular basis I receive emails and letters from people that I have met who tell me that they are either on their way to writing a book, getting into public speaking themselves, or even that they are just simply inspired to get back into their craft!

There is no real way to quantify or measure the power of creativity; its force is boundless and limitless.

Unleash the power of your creativity and watch your life and possibly the lives of those around you change...

KNOWLEDGE CHECK!

1. In your own words, what does the sentence "Creativity is the masterful wielding of the imagination on the physical world" mean to you?

2. Is there a real way to measure the power of creativity? If yes, please explain.

3. How can creativity make you or someone else's life better?

LESSON 5

How to overcome writer's block

In this lesson, you'll go on the most important mission of your life and kick open the door to your creativity, hog-tie and gag your inner-editor, blow the vault where he has locked away your most precious gift of all, your voice!!

HOW TO OVERCOME WRITER'S BLOCK

Write. Write anything. Turn off your inner-editor. Let it be. Let it be wack. Let it be great. Confess something. Offend someone. Inspire someone. Write a lie. Tell a truth. Tell yourself that everything you write is just another stair up towards your masterpiece. No matter what, just keep creating. Sometimes creating is like driving at night with dim headlights. You may not be able to see that far in front of you, but as long as you keep shining your lights ahead you'll get there.

This lesson is all about unblocking your creative flow! This is where we turn a chisel into a jackhammer and crack the vault wide open to take back your voice!

THESE 15-MINUTE WRITING EXERCISES WILL HELP YOU OVERCOME WRITER'S BLOCK.

Free Association – Begin by just letting the pen move on the paper, and as soon as words, ideas, or images come to mind write them down. If things stop coming to your mind throughout the 15 minutes simply go back to letting the pen move until they do. Then continue writing!

The Unsendable Letter – Write a letter to someone saying all the things you've never had the chance or opportunity to say. It could be to a crush, an ex lover, someone that cut you off in traffic, a family member, or even someone that has passed away.

Write anything. Turn off your inner-editor – Just write. Don't worry about the topic, spelling, coherency or legibility. Just Write.

Confess something – Write about something or several things you never told anyone. Tell as much or as little as you choose.

Offend someone – Write openly and honestly about your point of view on any subject you can think of, like religion, politics, you name it. Tell it like it is!!

Inspire someone – Write a note to someone that you admire or look up to.

Write a lie – Tell the craziest and most ridiculous lie you can think up.

Tell a truth – Name something that you know is a lie and why you know.

Turn the page. Don't censor yourself. Turn off your inner-editor and write.

FREE ASSOCIATION

THE UNSENDABLE LETTER

WRITE ANYTHING. TURN OFF YOUR INNER-EDITOR.

CONFESS SOMETHING.

OFFEND SOMEONE.

INSPIRE SOMEONE.

WRITE A LIE.

TELL A TRUTH.

BONUS LESSON

Write what you need to write!

"Before you can write what you want to write
you must first write what you need to write."

In my poetry workshops one of the first writings we do together is called
The Big Blue Sea Monster. The Big Blue Sea Monster is a metaphor for
our depression or maybe even somebody else's depression

Read the example and then write your own version!

THE BIG BLUE SEA MONSTER

Go ahead and fall

fall

fall

fall

deep down into that blue hole of self

where the weight of yesterday
and the high brick walls of tomorrow
are pressing you, crushing you flat

on your back, tirelessly

wringing out your tears like old rags and
smothering your desperate pleas into

quiet stillness

drag your tired body
up the mountain of the day

work, school, social function

(I watch my mask slide off
but I quickly prop it back up
with a forced smile, a swift glint
of the teeth)

then
run to sleep
escape to sleep
sleep all day and night to release
yourself from the big blue sea monster
drowning you as you weep and
sleep is not enough to get free
there is not enough sleep you can sleep to wake up
and snap out of it so

fall
fall
fall

fall some more

run from that big blue creep

crawl around in your funk
fall into the tv
tangle yourself in his sticky web for a week
pig out at the drive throughs
fall into your dark bedroom surrounded by gadgets and junk food wrappers

fall into the shame
that's brought on by the shame
of doing things that made you ashamed of yourself,

dance in that circle for a while,
get dizzy, get sick of it all
dance until you fall

you don't know why it's there
why it came in the first place
when it's going to leave
if it's going to leave

you watch the clock swing its bloody arms like swords as your goals zip by and cut
you off from life –it feels like you slowly die one day at a time but not all at once but
you still die, skip showers, meetings, work, sometimes sunlight, sometimes entire
weeks slip by in a wink and its time to show your face, lose the weight or shave or
pay bills
even though you don't wanna, ya gotta

cause that blue monster
kills you inside

it's hell
for a spell

so fall

for a season
it's ok

and when you're ready

when you've fought the blue beast off once more

come back

THE BIG BLUE SEA MONSTER

LESSON 6

Dissecting The Ninja Turtle Poem

In this lesson, you will learn about spoken word poetry, get an overview of the 5 stages of writing spoken word poetry, and learn how those 5 stages plus unification, message, and metaphor were applied to a poem that I wrote called The Ninja Turtle Poem.

"I saw the angel in the marble and carved until I set him free."

- Michelangelo

THE 5 STAGES
OF
WRITING SPOKEN WORD

1. BRAINSTORM

central idea for the poem/message and metaphor

2. ROUGH DRAFT

add more ideas and flesh out the body of the poem

3. FIRST DRAFT

tighten up unification, message and metaphor

4. FINAL DRAFT

finalize all of your ideas, call it done

5. MASTERPIECE

memorize poem

SPOKEN WORD

Spoken Word is a mixture of rhyme and free verse.
Free verse is poetry that does not rhyme or have a regular meter.

Spoken Word can be both rhyme and free verse, or it can be just free verse with no rhyme, or it can be all rhyme and no free verse. A Spoken Word poem can be any length that the writer chooses. Spoken Word is a form of poetry that is written with the intention of being recited or performed on any kind of stage in front of any kind of audience. Spoken Word is performance art.

Example

I am what I am

I am what I am
I am a product of the gutter
Its dirt, its hurt, its hopes and its dreams
I am its broken windows and its piles
upon piles of salvation army clothes
That bury my worth; I'm robed in...
I'm clothed in her catastrophic cloth
I am her hard-knock fashion faux pas
Strutting
      Running down the runway.
I am what I am
I'm a runner sometimes
A survivor
But I am not these rags
These clothes
These broken windows
I am the one
That sees the cycle
Determined to break it
Even if that brand of freedom means
My soul is homeless; naked
I am what I am
I am the one
                      that made it

THE NINJA TURTLE POEM | BRAINSTORM

central idea: a poem about the comparisons of the Ninja Turtles to my own childhood and things I learned as a father/mentor

message: children need their fathers

metaphor: the Ninja Turtles were much like me and my brothers

Below is a basic brainstorm. I jot down everything that comes to mind when I think of my central idea, message and metaphor.

Michelangelo Leonardo Raphael Donatello master splinter April O'Neil Casey jones renaissance painter sewers gutters ghettos heroes good people honor respect fathers mentors ghetto kids mutants teenagers at risk youth my son not having a dad raising a kid single parents fighting against the urge to be mad at the world enemies their traps shredder Krang bebop rock steady toys in cheap plastic good guys versus bad guys losing your identity and getting your self mixed up in a crowd choosing between becoming a villain or a hero kids need good parents and role models to help them choose the right path mentors are needed to guide kids towards the right path watching TV back in 4th grade and mom doing her best to raise her kids on her own growing up without a father its about finding your personal power no matter what you are going through in life and doing your best to overcome your obstacles look for heroes to look up to look for mentors to look up to don't abandon your child this poem is about my favorite super heroes and the importance of staying in your kids life and paying homage to my mentor

---

THE NINJA TURTLE POEM | ROUGH DRAFT
add more ideas and flesh out body of poem

Once upon a time in a gutter

I learned from Leonardo, Donatello, Raphael and Michelangelo

I learned basic things like just because your skin is a different color or you come from the gutter
doesn't mean that you have to keep your abilities or confidence undercover and   where you're
raised or where you're from has absolutely nothing to do with who you   are becoming and
everything to do with the super human strength that you possess to   overcome it

And April O'Neil in her bright yellow jump suit taught me that we have the power to
change the evening news and strip it of all it's darkness and blues

I also learned that Shredder and his cutting cutlery his Foot Clan his Bebops and
Rocksteady's are hiding everywhere in disguises like wolves in sheep's clothing

their traps are plenty

But the most important lesson that I learned from 4 mutants and a noble Rat is that a real man
stays in combat and raises his children up so that they don't go out into the world and re-
animate the life they are so heroically fighting to escape

You just need to fill a few homes with fathers Enter Master Splinter

Ya see, back in 4th grade at 4 o'clock-Ninja-star sharp everyday

I had T-shirts and action figures trapper keepers

My mother did her best

too easy for us young bucks to get the villains and hero's roles mixed up

children need fathers

THE NINJA TURTLE POEM | First Draft
tighten up unification message metaphor

Below I didn't write out the whole poem, but to give you an idea of tightening up unification, message, and metaphor I have highlighted words and ideas that connect to the message and metaphor.

Once upon a time while **fighting** my way out of the **gutter** it dawned on me that

everything I ever needed to know in life about being a man I learned from **Leonardo,**

Donatello, Raphael and Michelangelo. The Teenage Mutant Ninja Turtles I

learned basic things like just because your **skin is a different color** or you come from

the **gutter** doesn't mean that you have to keep your **abilities** or confidence undercover

and where you're raised or where you're from has absolutely nothing to do with who you

are becoming and everything to do with the **super human strength** that you possess to

overcome it You've got to overcome it! And **April O'Neil** in her bright yellow jump suit

taught me that we have the power to change the evening news, and strip it of all it's

darkness and blues, half truths and whole lies I also learned that **Shredder** and his

cutting cutlery, his **Foot Clan, his Bebops and Rocksteady's** are hiding everywhere

in disguises like wolves in sheep's clothing with plans to derail your plans and slowly pull

the wool over your eyes so stay wise because their traps are plenty But the most important

lesson that I learned from **4 mutants and a noble Rat** is that **a real man stays in**

combat and raises his children up so that they don't go out into the world

and re-animate the life they are so heroically fighting to escape...

THE NINJA TURTLE POEM | FINAL DRAFT
finalize all of your ideas, call it done

Once upon a time while fighting my way out of the gutter it dawned on me that everything I ever needed to know in life about being a man I learned from Leonardo, Donatello, Raphael and Michelangelo. **The Teenage Mutant Ninja Turtles** I learned basic things like just because your skin is a different color or you come from the gutter doesn't mean that you have to keep your *abilities or confidence undercover* and where you're **raised** or where you're **from** has absolutely nothing to do with who you are becoming and everything to do with the super human strength that you possess to overcome it **You've got to overcome it!** And April O'Neil in her bright yellow jump suit taught me that we have the power to change the evening news, and strip it of all it's darkness and blues, half truths and whole lies **I also learned that Shredder** and his cutting cutlery, his **Foot Clan, his Bebops and Rocksteady's** are hiding everywhere in disguises like wolves in sheep's clothing with plans to derail your plans and slowly pull the wool over your eyes so stay wise because their traps are plenty *But the most important lesson that I learned from 4 mutants and a noble Rat is that a real man stays in combat and raises his children up so that they don't go out into the world and re-animate the life they are so heroically fighting to escape you don't need guns you don't even really need capes You just need to fill a few homes with fathers* **Enter Master Splinter my first Mentor** He was everything I **never had and all that I wanted to be** He is the only father I knew and back then I never realized that I was gathering all the truth that **this animated rat gave me** what he taught stayed and by 9th grade Splinter came to life and manifested as my math Teacher, Mr. Chapin. No doubt about it he truly cared and that's what saved me. **Ya see, back in 4th grade at 4 o'clock-Ninja-star sharp everyday** my imagination was completely free to ooze underneath dank New York City streets on FOX TV. I was a fiend. I had everything from the **T-shirts and action figures to the video games and trapper keepers.** My mother did her best. But truth be told trying to raise a bunch of teenage mutants on your own in a fatherless home is a **wreck** plain and simple <u>**boys need fathers in order to become men.**</u> It's awful when we pretend. When we're left to fend for ourselves we begin to mimic **the synthetic polymer over polished toys in cheap plastic packaging** it's far too easy for us young bucks to get the villains and hero's roles **mixed up** and so transform into one **hell of a bastard.** Abandon your child? **Only a shell of a man would do something that dastardly!** So if you're in the **gutter in the sewer** fighting to make things right *then do what's right and stay in the fight* <u>**because the world needs its heroes**</u> **and the children need their fathers** and now that I'm grown with a child of my own I am giving my son EVE-RY-THING Everything I ever wanted! **Everything I always needed but never had** and that's a *mutant boy that became a deadbeat teenage father* and then <u>somehow someway turned it all around and</u> <u>miraculously</u> mutated into a **Dad**

This is a process that I suggest using as you work on your writing. It is helpful, but as you progress in your own writing you will abandon this method and develop what works best for you!

LESSON 7

Writing a spoken word poem from start to finish

In this lesson, you will write a spoken word poem from start to finish. Apply each phase of writing from brainstorm to final draft, and apply what you have learned from previous lessons to write a "good poem."

THE 5 STAGES
OF
WRITING SPOKEN WORD

1. BRAINSTORM

central idea for the poem/message and metaphor

2. ROUGH DRAFT

add more ideas and flesh out the body of the poem

3. FIRST DRAFT

tighten up unification, message and metaphor

4. FINAL DRAFT

finalize all of your ideas, call it done

5. MASTERPIECE

memorize poem

SPOKEN WORD BRAINSTORM

In the space provided below, begin your Spoken Word Brainstorm. Determine a **message** and a **metaphor** that you will use. Write freely all over the blank space or draw a circle with a **central idea** in the middle of it, and then draw other circles connected to the main circle with other related ideas in them, images, thoughts, scenes, smells etc.(spider web style)...

SPOKEN WORD ROUGH DRAFT

Here, you will begin fleshing out the body of your Spoken Word Poem by using the ideas that you came up with in the brainstorm.

SPOKEN WORD FIRST DRAFT

In the first draft of your Spoken Word Poem you want to tighten up the piece by unifying ideas, connecting words and ideas, and implanting the metaphors that tie into the central idea and message.

_____
_____
_____
_____
_____
_____
_____
_____
_____
_____
_____
_____
_____
_____
_____
_____
_____
_____
_____
_____
_____
_____
_____
_____
_____
_____
_____
_____

SPOKEN WORD FINAL DRAFT

Finalize the poem. All ideas and messages are finished.

_____
_____
_____
_____
_____
_____
_____
_____
_____
_____
_____
_____
_____
_____
_____
_____
_____
_____
_____
_____
_____
_____
_____
_____
_____
_____
_____
_____
_____
_____

MASTERPIECE

I have defined masterpiece as the moment when the performer can confidently recite their original work from memory and in front of a live audience.

You can memorize your poem by repetition and "exposure therapy".

Steps to Achieve Masterpiece.

1. Start by reading your poem aloud in front of a mirror 10 times or more for 3 days in a row. Practice implementing cadence, crescendo, and caesura into your recitation.

2. Then call up at least 10 friends and or family members and read it to them, ask for feedback. Listen to their feedback. If it's valuable to you, keep it. If you don't like it, then quietly throw it away…

3. After that, read the poem in front of at least 2 people. Ask one of them to hold a copy of your poem and follow along with you while you do your best to recite the poem from memory. Have them inform you when you have skipped a part or messed up in anyway. If you do mess up, start from the top and go over it until you don't mess up anymore.

4. Make it a performance! Command the space, command attention, make eye-contact, use body language!

5. Study and apply Section 3 of this book, "Confidence."

LESSON 8

Public Speaking 101: My Ninja Turtle TED Talk

In this lesson, you'll learn the very basics of how to formulate a short speech and deliver it confidently to a small audience.

PUBLIC SPEAKING 101: THE NINJA TURTLE TED TALK

A universal and personal message

Beginning: Create a <u>universal message</u> here; one that the majority of your audience can relate to.

As kids, we all watched cartoons and identified with super heroes on some level. Whether it was Super Man or Wonder Woman, our wild and free imaginations found characteristics inside these special people that we wished to have in ourselves in some way. The ability to fly, x-ray vision, moving objects with our minds, you name it! We truly believed that super human ability was possible. That's what being a child was all about! Super heroes were our first role models, after parents of course!

Middle: This is where you want to begin making your <u>message personal</u>.

My father passed away when I was 3 years old from a self-inflicted gunshot wound, he committed suicide. This sent my mother into a deep depression and she found drugs, alcohol and writing poetry as her only means of self-medication. Sadly the drugs and alcohol took her life over, leaving poetry on the back burner. My mother is without a doubt my first super hero because even though she succumbed to addiction, she did the very best she could to raise 3 boys on her own, and she introduced me to poetry. After raising just 1 boy with help, I knew it took tremendous super human strength to raise a child let alone 3 and on your own at that. My second super hero or heroes (role models) were a lot of kids first heroes too, the Teenage Mutant Ninja Turtles! I had so much in common with them: They loved pizza, so did I. They were raised by a single parent, so was I. Their layer was the sewer or "the gutter", and mine was the ghetto. They were a different color than everyone else; I was often the only black kid in most of my schools. Most importantly despite coming from the bottom and against all odds they still chose to go out into the world and do what's right. They kept their honor and looked out for others as well as each other.

End: Here you will just <u>rephrase your universal and personal messages</u> to conclude your short speech. Maybe even throw in a favorite quote to summarize your message.

My mentor or "Master Splinter" once told me that "tough times come and go, tough people stay". Heroes are tough. If you are reading this or hearing this today then you are unquestionably a hero made of the same "tough stuff" that your favorite childhood heroes are made from. Now go out there and make the world a better place... oh yeah and eat some pizza while you're at it!

WRITE A SHORT 2-MINUTE SPEECH OF YOUR OWN.

This was just a short example of a 10-minute talk that I do for educators and struggling urban youths. The same rules apply to public speaking as they do to poetry and or rap. Does it communicate? Is there unification, a message, and a little creativity or metaphor?

The very first writing in this book is on page 8 called Introduce Yourself in 100 words. It asks where you're from, where you're at, and where you're going. Here is your next assignment. In the space provided below, rewrite that introduction of yourself into a short 2-minute speech or write a short speech that talks about the story behind the spoken word poem that you have written similar to my "Ninja Turtle TED Talk".

_____

_____

_____

_____

_____

_____

_____

_____

_____

_____

_____

_____

_____

_____

_____

_____

_____

_____

_____

_____

_____

Let's brush up on our communication skills from Section 1 of this book, expand them, and apply them to Public Speaking 101.

5 MINUTES TO TELEPATHY ON AN AUDIENCE

THE PURPOSE:

To practice confident eye contact with an audience and deliver a short 2-minute speech or back story to a spoken word poem.

THE IDEA:

1 person (the speaker) stands in front of 2 or more seated people and completes the following timed exercises to the best of their abilities, then they deliver a short 2-minute speech.

YOU WILL NEED:

3 people, 2 chairs, and a timer. Throughout the following exercises the speaker will stand about 5 feet in front of 2 or more seated people. The speaker will distribute eye contact evenly amongst the audience.

INSTRUCTIONS:

Level 1. Confident-silent-eye-contact with an audience –stand and make confident-silent-eye-contact with an audience for 60 seconds.

Level 2. Gibberish with an audience –speak in a made up language or gibberish with an audience for 60 seconds.

Level 3. Small talk with an audience –have a conversation about anything you choose with the audience for 60 seconds.

Level 4. Deliver your 2-minute speech –deliver the 2-minute speech you wrote earlier in this lesson to the audience.

Public Speaking is said to be the #1 fear next to dying. Can you believe that? We will discuss fear more in the next section of this workbook!

Spoken Word & Public Speaking 101 Review

1. What is Spoken Word?

_____

_____

_____

2. What are the 5 phases of writing a Spoken Word Poem in this workbook?

_____

_____

_____

3. When preparing a short speech what should the intro have in it?

_____

_____

4. What is one thing that both poetry and a short speech have in common?

_____

_____

5. What is the #1 fear next to dying? In your own words, write down why you think that is...

_____

_____

_____

_____

_____

_____

REAL WORLD CHALLENGE!

Knowledge and Application make up 360° of education. In this challenge, apply what you have learned from this section.

1. Memorize your spoken word poem from this section.

2. Call a friend or family member and read it to them.

3. Practice reciting your poem to someone while making eye contact.

SECTION 2 WRAP UP...

Now that you have written a spoken word poem and learned a few things about public speaking, lets move on to the final section and load up on the ingredient that makes it all happen, confidence!

3

CONFIDENCE

WHAT IS CONFIDENCE?

When my son first came to live with me in the 5th grade he was very shy, overweight, and insecure. In the summertime, he grew his hair out and would wear a zip up sweater that had a hoodie on it, a security blanket of sorts. He hid his talents, abilities, and personality behind his growing low self-esteem.

In the first month of him living with me I asked my son what he wanted to be when he grew up. He told me that he wanted to be a rapper, so the very next day we went out and bought a dictionary. His goal was to write down and define at least 10 new words a day to build up his vocabulary and increase communication power.

Next, I enrolled him into a youth improv class at the local Academy of Children's Theater. There he learned to be comfortable in the spotlight, think on his feet, and exercise his vocabulary. We eventually bought a laptop and microphone so he could begin to record his music.

With every song he wrote his confidence soared to greater heights.

Making art builds confidence!

Over the course of the first year of him living with me, he wrote at least 10 original songs, cut his hair, lost weight, and came all the way out of his shell. Art saves lives. Art builds confidence. Confidence is self-love in the highest sense of the idea. If you truly like yourself you will pursue your dreams, you will take care of yourself, you will protect yourself and your dreams from anything that threatens their prosperity.

Here I ask: do you like yourself?

CONFIDENCE is SELF—LOVE

KNOWLEDGE CHECK!

1. What is confidence?

2. What will "making art" help build?

3. In the short essay about confidence, what experiences helped my son come "all the way out of his shell"?

Before proceeding to the next lesson, write 100 things that you like about yourself in the boxes below.

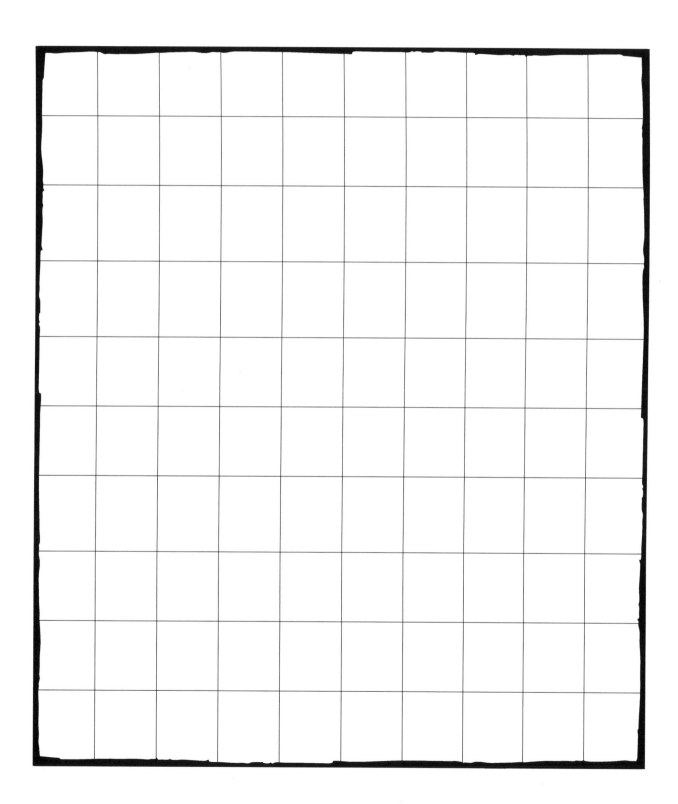

LESSON 9

Storytelling & Improv:
Turning stage fright into stage courage

In this lesson, you will learn why you should have the
confidence to perform no matter what. You will also learn a few
basic improv games that will help you overcome your fear of
performing in front of a live audience.

THE THREE REASONS WHY YOU SHOULD PERFORM NO MATTER WHAT!

1. There will be someone in the audience that believes they can do a better job than you. They will now try. You will have <u>inspired</u> them.

2. There will be someone in the audience that believes that they are not as good as you. They will now try. You will have <u>inspired</u> them.

3. There will be someone in the audience that has no desire to be better than you or to even try, they will be <u>inspired</u> by your sheer courage to share your art.

That's what it all comes down to in the end, overcoming whatever it is that is blocking you from getting up and sharing your art and inspiring others.

STORYTELLING & IMPROV

Poets are storytellers.

Poets, performers, and public speakers alike are not only storytellers but are also (and sometimes have to be) actors or improvisational artists. They have to be able to think on their feet and go with the flow of whatever happens while speaking and/or performing on stage.

Storytelling & Improv are vital to the Art of the Spoken Word because often we like to go on stage with a plan, and that plan can easily blow up in our face due to stage fright, a heckler, you name it!

The last thing we want, after all the hard work we put into our writing, is to look like a foolish amateur that's new to the stage!

Learning a few improv basics will help you think on your feet and overcome unexpected situations that can occur and most likely will occur if you choose to stick with the craft long enough.

The 2 words that guide an improv artist's life on stage are.

"Yes and..."

"Yes and" are words of agreement, flow, and contribution.

Saying "yes" to a moment rather than resisting the moment allows you to be flexible and at ease, playful even.

The "and" part opens the door for you to agree with and respond positively to what's coming your way, while adding your own personal touch to that moment.

For example: lets say you're on stage and someone shouts "POETRY SUCKS!!" That could be a nightmare for you if you suffer from stage fright or it's your first public performance! Rather than responding with negativity and resistance to the moment you could simply say yes to the moment

"Yes! Poetry does suck... the boredom out of everyday life!"

and then continue with your recitation or talk without being defeated by shock or embarrassment. Or you could even ignore it and continue on.

That was a very basic example of saying "yes and..." to a very stressful moment.

Have you ever been in a heated argument with someone and then after you leave the battle you think of all the things you should've and could've said?
Notice how after you've walked away and cooled down all the right words and comebacks seem to magically come to mind?

The French have a phrase for that **"The wit of the staircase."**

To get to the point where your wit is sharp enough to respond in such a way takes a lot of practice, experience, and self-confidence.

The reason why you weren't able to respond how you wanted to in the moment is due to what Daniel Goleman, author of Emotional Intelligence, calls "amygdala hi-jacking" or "emotional hi-jacking". It's when you are taken off-guard by an imagined threat. You respond emotionally rather than logically to the moment.

A few pages ahead are a couple of improv games that I have learned over the years that have helped me strengthen my "yes and..." muscle.

But before we jump into those games let's talk about the very foe, the big bad bully that defeats us before we even step foot on stage. Fear!!

FEAR

Fear is basically a feeling of anxiety or stress caused by imagining the outcome of a circumstance not going our way.

The key word here is *imagining*. You can control your imagination.

If you fantasize your performance going horribly it will go that way.
If you fantasize your performance going great it will go that way.

Here's my second most favorite acronym from the word fear:
Fantasizing Events Appearing Real.

Sometimes most of what we fear is the negative fantasy that we are visualizing and quite possibly creating for ourselves. Practice visualizing your performance going according to plan, make this a pre-show ritual and watch your anxiety begin to shrink.

My absolute most favorite acronym from the word fear is:
Face Everything And Recover.

In the last 4 years I have performed for and/or spoken to well over 250,000 people by my estimation, and every time I took the stage I became nervous, anxious, and fearful. But by facing the moment head on and recovering from it, my fear dwindled and I became a little more confident each time.

There have been times where I have forgotten my lines, felt that I was perspiring too much, stuttered too much, sounded like a fool, felt stiff and uncomfortable in my body, unprepared, you name it! But every time I overcame it!

Turn your stage fright into stage courage by choosing to face everything that comes your way!

KNOW YOUR FEAR!

What happens to you when you fear speaking in front of people?

Me?

My stomach gets a wave of anxiety. I sweat and sometimes stumble my words.

Do you know what happens to you when you get nervous? What are some of your reactions when you know you have to speak in front of people?

List them below:

_____

_____

_____

_____

_____

_____

_____

Just knowing that these things are going to arise when its time to speak or perform will help you overcome them. Plan for them. Expect them. And prepare to overcome them. I do a few breathing and visualization exercises to help me overcome the wave of anxiety. I also keep a handkerchief for sweat and a bottle of water to keep my mouth from going dry which causes me to stumble my words.

Below write a few things that you can do to help you overcome your nervous reactions.

_____

_____

_____

_____

_____

_____

_____

_____

ULTIMATELY, THIS IS WHAT I'VE LEARNED ABOUT THE ENEMY, FEAR...

Fear never actually goes away, you learn its characteristics, its patterns, you become well acquainted with fear's fragrances and body odors, as you have your siblings, enemies, lovers, and friends. You come to know fear and defeat it, though you can never really kill fear, fear is immortal and invincible, but the good news is, SO ARE YOU! And when you defeat fear you must bestow upon it forgiveness and grace, for fear is an enemy that you defeat by befriending.

The following exercises will help you think on your feet and go with the flow of the moment all while strengthening your stage courage and confidence.

IT WAS A DARK AND STORMY NIGHT...

THE PURPOSE:

This is an improv story building exercise designed to help the performer/speaker say "yes and..." to the moment, think on his or her feet, go with the flow, and gain stage courage and confidence. This exercise also helps with memorizing lines.

HOW TO PLAY:

2 or more people sit across from each other or in a circle and build a story together.

The first person begins with the line

"It was a dark and stormy night...".

The second person must repeat the first line and add another part of the story to it like this:

"It was a dark and stormy night and a large white owl perched himself upon a hollow tree."

Now the first person or, the third person (depending on however many people you have playing) goes again and repeats everything that has been said and adds to it:

"It was a dark and stormy night and a large white owl perched himself upon a hollow tree and watched as a lonely traveler moved eerily through the cool white fog..."

OBJECT OF THE GAME:

Build a story that's at least 20 lines long. Each player must repeat each line that has been said. No player can change anything that has been said, meaning the player must agree and contribute (or say "yes and...") to the story.

Players should do their best to unify and bring the story full circle!

WIT OF THE STAIRCASE

THE PURPOSE:

The purpose of this game is to help the performer/speaker think on their feet, overcome being emotionally hi-jacked, and ultimately handle the anxiety that comes with being put on the spot.

HOW TO PLAY:

2 people stand approximately 3 feet apart facing each other. Person A asks Person B a question, Person B must answer Person A with a question and Person A must again answer Person B with a question...

RULES:

1. You cannot answer any part of the question
2. You cannot repeat a question that has been asked
3. You cannot pause for longer than 5 seconds
4. You cannot talk over the other player

OBJECT OF THE GAME:

Players must ask each other questions until they both feel that they are thinking on their feet and do not feel emotionally hi-jacked. It will be personal resolution.

VARIATIONS:

To make the game more challenging, choose a location or theme such as only asking questions that pertain to the beach or maybe outer space. If a player asks a question outside of these locations or themes they lose.

STORYTELLING & IMPROV REVIEW

1. What are the 2 words that guide an improv artist's life on stage?

_____

_____

2. What are the 2 different acronyms for fear listed in this lesson?

_____

_____

_____

_____

3. How does one turn stage fright into stage courage?

_____

_____

_____

4. What is fear?

_____

_____

_____

_____

5. Does fear actually ever go away? Please explain...

_____

_____

_____

_____

_____

LESSON 10

Masks & Animation

In this lesson, you will learn Stage Presence and how to become more comfortable in your own skin. You'll also create an alter-ego that will help you put more life and confidence into your performance.

MASKS & ANIMATION
facial and body language exercise

THE PURPOSE:

To become comfortable in your own skin through five 1-minute playful exercises in facial expression and body movement so that you, the performer/speaker, are aware that face and body also communicate.

THE IDEA:

Two people stand about 2 feet apart from one another with plenty of room behind them and to their sides for movement. The exercises are designed so that the participants become comfortable with their face and body being the center of attention and to gain the awareness that our facial expressions and body language communicate.

YOU WILL NEED:

2 people, enough space to move around freely, and a timer.

INSTRUCTIONS:

Level 1. Masks – Person A makes as many different facial expressions as they wish, Person B mirrors each facial expression for 60 seconds.

Level 2. Masks – Person B takes the lead for 60 seconds, Person A mirrors.

Level 3. Masks & Animation – Person A makes as many facial expressions and body movements as they wish, Person B mirrors each facial expression and body movement for 60 seconds.

Level 4. Masks & Animation – Person B takes the lead for 60 seconds, Person A mirrors.

Level 5. Masks, Animation, and Conversation – Person A and Person B take turns mirroring facial expressions and body movements while holding a conversation for 60 seconds.

MASKS & ANIMATION
creating an alter-ego for performance

Man is LEAST himself when he talks in his own person.
Give him a mask and he will tell you the truth. -Oscar Wilde

THE PURPOSE:

This is a lesson in ALTER-EGOism.

The purpose of this lesson is to get the performer to step outside
of their comfort zone, breathe life into their words, and create a performance that
captivates and inspires audiences.

Mask (noun)

A covering for all or parts of the face, in particular: a covering worn as a disguise, or
to amuse or terrify other people

Animation (noun)

The state of being full of life or vigor; liveliness, the state of being alive

Alter Ego (noun)

A person's secondary or alternative personality, an intimate and trusted friend

Developing an alter-ego helps to create distance between who you have learned to become and the personality/ performer you will learn to breathe life into.

Step 1. Take your first and last name and come up with a new name, an alter ego name that you will give your mask.

Step 2. Create a mask using construction paper, scissors, acrylic paint, and whatever you can find.

Step 3. Answer the questions on mask personality profile on the next page. Give it life!

Step 4. Create movement unique to this character: glances, stares, awkward body movements, quirks etc. Be as strange as possible, get out of your comfort zone!

Step 5. Questions and answers with your mask. Stand in front of the room and introduce your mask to a person or group of people. Allow them to ask questions and you answer them from the mask's perspective.

MASK PERSONALITY PROFILE

Answer the following questions from the
perspective of your mask's personality

1. What is your name?

2. Where are you from? Name of home planet?

3. How old are you?

4. What is your favorite food?

5. What secrets of the universe do you know?

6. Where did you get that scar?

7. What is the meaning of love?

8. What powers or abilities do you posses?

9. What is the most interesting thing that has ever happened to you?

10. What color is your skin?

11. What gets you into trouble?

ALTER-EGO PERFORMANCE
WITH STAGE PRESENCE

Perform your Spoken Word Poem
as the alter-ego that you created
to yourself in front of a mirror.

Be sure to...

1.   Command the space
2.   Command attention
3.   Make eye-contact
4.   Use body language

MASKS & ANIMATION REVIEW

1. What is an alter-ego?

_____

_____

_____

2. What 4 things make stage presence?

_____

_____

_____

_____

3. What does developing an alter-ego help with?

_____

_____

_____

_____

_____

LESSON 11

Vocal warm-ups and body warm-ups
Pre-show rituals

In this lesson, you will learn a few things that will
help you prepare for your on-stage performance.

VOCAL WARM-UPS AND BODY WARM-UPS

The following are a few vocal warm-ups and body
warm-ups I use myself or with a group of students or performers.

Lick your teeth – With your mouth closed, lick the outside of your teeth. Go left for ten circles and then right for ten circles. You will begin to feel your jaw and temple muscles become sore, this is normal.

O-E-O-E – While staring down at the floor say the letter O as long and as drawn out as possible, your mouth should be open as wide as possible. This will also relieve some of the tension built up from licking your teeth. Right after saying O, you then say the letter E as long and as drawn out as possible. You should almost be making a "say cheese" kind of smile while saying E.
Repeat saying O and E over and over and eventually speed up saying O and E faster and faster until you run out of wind. Then repeat this warm-up again but this time stare at the ceiling. This will help loosen up your vocal cords.

A big black bug – Repeat the following phrase over and over again until you can do it without messing up.

A big black bug bit a big black bear and made a big black bear bleed blood.

I need New York – Repeat the following phrase over and over again until you can do it with out messing up.

I need New York, you need New York, I know you need unique New York.

Put your left foot in – Stick your left foot in front of you and shake it, then your left arm, then your right arm, then your head, shake everything up. Then, stick your right foot in front of you and shake it, then your right arm, then your left arm, then your head again, shake everything up!

Slow motion space exploration – In a private space and moving as slowly as possible swim through the air, and float around the room. Do your best to not touch anything or anyone in the room you are exploring.

Once you have completed each of the above vocal and body warm-ups, recite your spoken word poem from memory.

PRE-SHOW RITUALS

1. Do all of the vocal warm-ups.

2. Visualize your entire performance from the time you walk up to the stage to 5 minutes after you finish.

3. Visualize the audience applauding and supporting you.

4. Visualize yourself from the audience's point of view. See yourself on stage performing with courage and confidence

5. Do the "Put your left foot in" body warm-up to loosen up and to release tension

6. Recite your poem as fast as you can from memory.

7. Recite your poem at normal speed from memory.

8. Do some or all of these. It's up to you.

LESSON 12

The Capstone:
Perform in front of a live audience

In this lesson, you will apply everything you learned in this workbook and perform in front of a live audience.

THE CAPSTONE

The dictionary's definition of a capstone is 'a stone fixed on top of something' such as a wall or a tomb.

Remember in the beginning of this workbook we compared the attainment of knowledge similar to building a Pyramid.

The capstone will be the final mud-brick set in that process. The ultimate goal of this workbook is to get you to the point where you can perform confidently in front of an audience. This is the final mud-brick in demonstrating all the knowledge and skills learned in the 12 lessons.

On the next few pages there are 4 final exercises to complete, a reflection essay to write, and then you will be given your final mission.

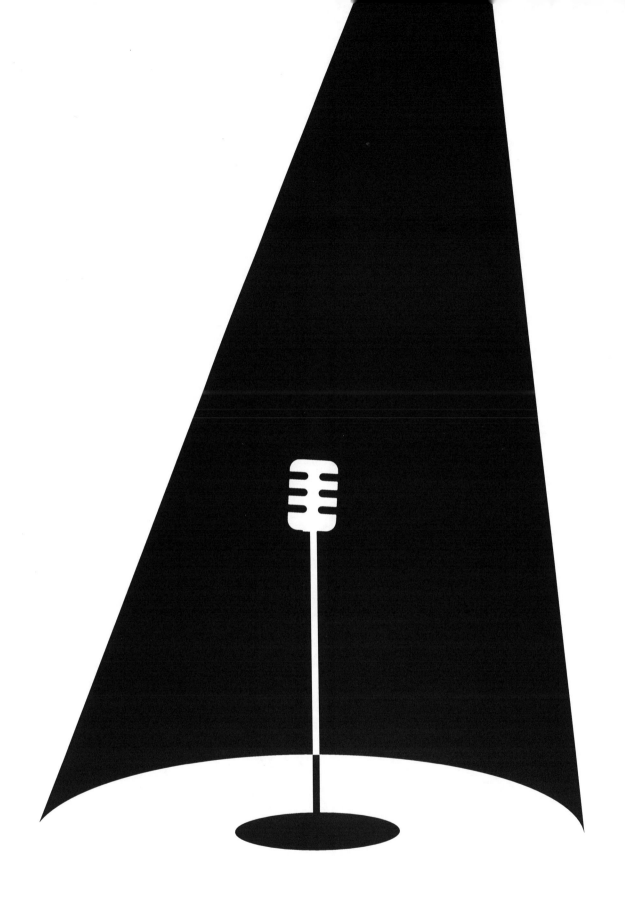

PERFORMER VS. AUDIENCE

THE PURPOSE:

To give the performer experience with different scenarios that he or she could experience while performing in front of a live audience.

THE IDEA:

(Use your Spoken Word poem for this exercise) 1 person is a speaker, the other person is the audience member. Both participants take turns being each of the roles below for 1 minute each.

Nervous performer reads to a rude audience
1. Person A reads their poem in front of the audience and stutters, shakes, and pretends to be very nervous.
2. Person B talks loud, plays with phone, and walks around room.
3. Person A and Person B switch roles.

Confident performer reads to a rude audience
4. Person A reads their poem with head up high while making eye contact.
5. Person B talks aloud, plays with phone, and walks around room.
6. Person A and Person B switch roles.

Nervous performer reads to a supportive audience
7. Person A reads their poem in front of audience and stutters, shakes, and pretends to be very nervous.
8. Person B listens politely until performer finishes then applauds.
9. Person A and Person B switch roles.

Confident performer reads to a supportive audience
10. Person A reads their poem with head up high while making eye contact.
11. Person B listens politely until performer finishes then applauds.
12. Person A and Person B switch roles.

ART OF THE SPOKEN WORD REFLECTION

Go back and briefly review each lesson in this book, and then write for 25 minutes about all you've learned and how these lessons will help you in performance and public speaking.

_____

_____

_____

_____

_____

_____

_____

_____

_____

_____

_____

_____

_____

_____

_____

_____

_____

_____

_____

_____

_____

_____

_____

_____

_____

_____

_____

_____

the end.

FINAL MISSION

Find an open-mic in your area and perform your Spoken Word poem for a live audience!

Apply everything that you've learned from this workbook!

FINAL WORD

I have dedicated the last ten years of my dreaming life to poetry and public speaking. And because of that countless doors have opened and continue to open for me. It is quite humbling to be asked to speak or perform for people.

Whether it's an elementary school, a college, a winery, a wedding, or a prison, I am truly honored to even be considered to speak or perform for them.

My friend Andy Perdue, a writer for the Seattle Times, dubbed me the "Poet Laureate of Northwest Wine Country". Patricia Briggs, a New York Times Best Selling Author, wrote a foreword in my second book of poetry. Academy Award Winner TJ Martin and World Famous Painter David Garibaldi said some pretty incredible things about my work as well. I have traveled to Athens, Greece, the Pyramids in Mexico, Big Sur, California and not to mention all 4 corners of the United States chasing my dream.

There is no greater feeling in life than your dream feeding you.

I have learned that magic happens when you give yourself fully to your passion, no matter what that passion happens to be.

This workbook was written to assist not just aspiring wordsmiths but my fellow dreamers out there as well. Communication, creativity, and confidence will help anyone in any pursuit. So this workbook is for you and anyone that you come across.

I am a poet, these lessons made my dreams come true, whatever your passion is pursue it and the same will happen for you…

PERSONAL JOURNAL

JOURNAL ENTRY | free write for 15 minutes or until entire page is filled up

JOURNAL ENTRY | free write for 15 minutes or until entire page is filled up

JOURNAL ENTRY | free write for 15 minutes or until entire page is filled up

JOURNAL ENTRY | free write for 15 minutes or until entire page is filled up

JOURNAL ENTRY | free write for 15 minutes or until entire page is filled up

JOURNAL ENTRY | free write for 15 minutes or until entire page is filled up

JOURNAL ENTRY | free write for 15 minutes or until entire page is filled up

JOURNAL ENTRY | free write for 15 minutes or until entire page is filled up

JOURNAL ENTRY | free write for 15 minutes or until entire page is filled up

JOURNAL ENTRY | free write for 15 minutes or until entire page is filled up

JOURNAL ENTRY | free write for 15 minutes or until entire page is filled up

JOURNAL ENTRY | free write for 15 minutes or until entire page is filled up

JORDAN CHANEY IS A SPOKEN WORD POET, AUTHOR, PUBLIC SPEAKER, TEACHER, MENTOR AND ALL-AROUND CREATIVE RESIDING IN EASTERN WASHINGTON'S WINE COUNTRY.

He is the author of *Art of the Spoken Word* – a workbook for enhancing communication skills, creativity, and confidence. He has published two poetry collections: *Rocket Fuel for Dreamers*, a poetry book about love and manifesting one's dreams, and *Double-Barreled Bible*, a collection of urban poems that blend Eastern and Western philosophies. He has also written a children's book, *M.C. Seuss: Once Upon a Rhyme*.

Most recently, he created Urban Poets Society, a youth-leadership program that promotes arts, literacy, and leadership in his community. He currently teaches a performance poetry and communications class at a local Juvenile Detention Center, where he helps youth find their voice through the power of poetry.

To book Jordan Chaney for speaking engagements, poetry workshops, performances and other events he can be contacted at:

jordanchaneypoet@gmail.com

facebook.com/jordanchaney

www.poetjordan.com

55403534R00105

Made in the USA
Charleston, SC
27 April 2016